Goodbye Self-Critical, Hello Self-Thrilled!

An Inspirational Tale of Healing and Empowerment

Joyce Anderson

ISBN:
978-0-9962133-0-1 *(First Edition)*
978-0-9962133-1-8 *(Second Edition 2020)*
978-0-9962133-2-5 *(e-book)*

Library of Congress Control Number: 2009914332

SEL023000 SELF-HELP / Personal Growth / Self-Esteem
SEL042000 SELF-HELP / Emotions
JNF053160 JUVENILE NONFICTION / Social Topics / Self-Esteem & Self-Reliance

For

Michael, Niki and Dylan who
are in every breath of my life

In memory of Gayle Anderson,
a beautiful writer

"A modern-day fairy tale–cum–allegory of self-actualization, healing and empowerment.

The hero's journey: that time-honored device for teaching truths about human development and existence. Anderson puts a feminine twist on this model in her debut novel, named for the two opposing, ultimately reconciling forces in the life of Agatha, the young protagonist. She enters this world, as do all children in Anderson's vision, radiating brilliant colors and delighting in her exuberant, unique gifts. She is an irresistible target for Conred, an otherworldly being who feeds on colors and leaves in their stead a pair of soldiers charged with imprisoning Agatha in grayness that defines Conred's existence. She goes from being boundlessly creative to being overweight and unhappily married— until Conred reappears. After he threatens her daughter, Zeal, Agatha meets Tellaga and learns the truth about both herself and Conred. With Tellaga's help, Agatha rediscovers the beauty of her being, the power of her gifts and the fierce, transformative power of compassion. It's an unabashed inspirational tale that enmeshes symbolic names and predictable plot twists with wildly inspired details, such as Zeal's talent for arranging inanimate objects into fanciful figures and scenes. Anderson delivers her story with earnest clarity, simplicity and straightforwardness, and she includes a study guide for readers who wish to apply Agatha's lessons to their own experiences. The hero starts out young, innocent and pure but encounters challenges as she battles to awaken her full potential. The tale is both an allegory for damaging a spirit, which so often occurs in childhood and beyond, as well as a methodology for neutralizing and overcoming the trauma.

A quick read and a reminder that the greatest prison—and its key—lies within."

Kirkus Review

Table of Contents

Table of Contents 4

Chapter 1: Agatha: "Who wouldn't love me?" 1

Chapter 2: Conred...9

Chapter 3: Conred and Agatha: "Who could possibly love me? ".. 15

Chapter 4: Logical Agatha 25

Chapter 5: Coates to the Rescue... 29

Chapter 6: Zeal: the Mundane into the Extraordinary..... 33

Chapter 7: Zeal's Pause... 44

Chapter 8: Tellaga.. 53

Chapter 9: Extra-ordinary Agatha 61

Chapter 10: Conred Ready 73

Chapter 11: Conred's Story 83

How this book came to be…... 100

How you can work with these archetypes:........................ 109

Reading Group Suggestions... 119

Joyce Anderson.. 123

Liz Gill Neilson 125

Chapter 1

Agatha: "Who wouldn't love me?"

I n her first days of sweet life, Agatha discovers her round, wonderful belly, the hub of her world. This magical belly never ceases to signal her desires. And from this magical center, her arms, hands, legs, and feet extend to accommodate her wheel of wishes. With agility she can put a hand or a foot in her mouth. When Agatha's body makes a noise or a funny output, she gets a loving response to aid in her comfort. There is a world answering to her desires. Her mother's arms would cradle, feed, and wash her. Her mother's voice would soothe her, and Agatha's heart would soar.

True to a little girl, Agatha's mother colored her room in pink, and dressed her in many different shades of pink. This was just fine by Agatha as she loved the color. She felt pink was the color of play. Agatha knew well about pure feelings and love. This feeling of love she experienced from the outside world matched her feelings inside. Her body and feelings got her what she wanted, and she thrived in the full thought of "Who wouldn't love me?" Now was delicious! Now was magical! Now was Agatha.

As a preschooler, her imagination and the world she created were endless. Agatha had the ability to create magnificent stories wherever she was, for any situation. Whoever received her stories would get the privilege of being weaved into the plot, spicing it up with humor and colorful images. The listener might be the hero engaged in rescuing another or the villain scheming up the dastardly plot. Her mother was her favorite fan. Agatha knew just when her mother needed a good escape and a laugh. Whenever she saw her mother look hard and concrete, a story would come through. After the telling, she saw her mother become supple and available. She sensed that her stories not only entertained but also soothed whoever listened, and many people did.

Ah, the magic of story! This was Agatha's born talent. Agatha could tell when a new story was about to be born, because her belly and heart would feel like butterflies tickling her. She knew to listen and make way for the new adventure coming through. She enthusiastically shared her stories every day while playing with her friends, who had their own talents. Joyce loved to sing and would accompany Agatha as she told her stories. Bonnie's talent was to boss them all around because she did it so well. Bonnie could always see who did the best at what, and she made sure that everyone stepped up to the plate. She would direct the play-of-the-day. As tough as he was, Rocky loved to count and do math. He made sure that everybody fit in and things always worked out. Stephen loved Legos and would always bring along his latest creation – he favored building monsters. Dora was very quiet and came to play shyly, with crayons and paper in hand. The kids couldn't wait to see what she had drawn. She created funny cartoons of each of them. And finally there was Marcel, who could play the violin from a very early age. Marcel's parents had great hope for his future, since they believed his talent was better than most.

But the children didn't compare their talents; they didn't know about that. They just knew that each would come to play with what they loved to do most. This was such a pure time for Agatha. To be around all her friends who freely displayed their favorite way to be, and they in turn hearing her way. Agatha felt special and welcome with her friends and at home. Each day, curious anticipation filled her heart.

But alas, when Agatha started her first year of school her world changed. Her feelings of "who wouldn't love me?" gradually changed to "who could possibly love me?" For when she turned five, her caring parents slowly became worried and angry parents. Their marriage was crumbling, and their anger in the present and their fear of the future scared them, and in turn affected Agatha. They argued over money and were dissatisfied with everything they thought wasn't right with the world. They dug into each other's skimpy container of self worth to fill their own. But this never worked. When their reserves were empty, their view of the world became unfriendly and stingy. Although they were scared, they acted as if they weren't. For their protection, they wore the costumes of "shoulds" that they thought were true. "I should only have friends that are good, God- fearing Christians." "I should fit in and not make waves." "I should agree with people so they won't be uncomfortable." "I should be liked." "I should be popular." "I should have a great car."

"I should not complain in public." "I should put others' needs first." "I should do the chores first and have fun only if there is time." "I should work for a large company so I will always have a salary, and they will tell me what to do." The "shoulds" went on and on.

Agatha's father would tell her not to worry, but this would make her very confused. "Be grateful for what we have, because there's not enough in the world," he would preach. Yet her home was filled with worry about that very thing! Her father couldn't understand why he couldn't get ahead at work; he did everything they expected, even at the expense of his own tastes and ideas. "Perhaps," he would mutter, "I will try harder to fit their mold so I can get the next promotion." But he feared that any promotion would always go to someone better than him. He wore this belief daily, and it made him angry deep down inside.

This is the man Agatha's mother greeted each day when he came home. Agatha's beautiful mother gave up the possibility of a career in opera when she got married. She realized that following that dream would be selfish and not a necessity in life. Agatha's mother and father were children of parents who lost everything in the Great Depression, which taught them that necessity was the guiding principle for everything. Being a good, sacrificing mother was the call of the day. Talents were only a luxury to be used after putting food on the table. Instead of using their special gifts in life, Agatha's parents found safety in large groups – lots of people pretending to believe the same thing. Her father worked for a huge corporation whose every employee believed their company was the best. They were members of a church with a large congregation all believing their religion was right. They lived in a large, white, barely-hanging-on, middle- class suburb that clung to the safety of common thoughts.

Since they had no time for their true talents, they found safety in being the same. They began to warn Agatha of the dangers in the world where things weren't all the same.

This world had no time for dreamers. "Agatha, it's not safe out there. There are thieves, murderers, and war. And worst of all, there are people who don't go to church," her father would warn.

Her parents' modeling of adulthood conveyed their philosophy to Agatha loud and clear: In order for the world to enjoy you, you must do what the world expects. If you don't do it, and don't do it well, you will not be welcome. And never forget how dangerous it is!

Agatha didn't like those warnings; they didn't match her belly and they hurt her heart. All that caution took up too much space in her body, and there started to be no room for Agatha. Her dependable belly that guided her daily didn't believe those warnings, and her belly let her hear about it. Out of love and loyalty to her parent's beliefs, Agatha started to pad her belly to keep it from screaming at her. She started eating more. Plus, this would make her bigger. Maybe she could make enough space to house all those warnings from her parents and still find room for Agatha. After all, she loved her parents, and they must know best. But her belly did not agree with what she was being taught. It was never silenced; it never gave up. Her hub kept screaming at her. She continued padding her belly and ignoring its guidance.

Thankfully she still found great solace and joy in her imagination and would often escape to her gift of story.

Goodbye Self-Critical, Hello Self-Thrilled!

Agatha was motivated to keep her stories alive as her first day of school was just around the corner. How fabulous to think there was a building that would supply her with even more interesting friends, all the same age, learning together – a place for her to share and fuel her stories. However, when the day of school finally did arrive, her great escape was soon to be threatened.

Chapter 2

Conred

Hovering above this worried world was an enormous energy, a real boogey man. He was not just the boogey man that stayed under beds at night, but one that shadowed the entire land – Conred, King of Comparison. His guiding principle for his kingdom: *Compare for Self Worth, for then there will be none.* What an insidious King he was, with a kingdom that stretched across the world. His weapon was the Shade of Gray, and it had but one purpose – to kill originality. Originality cannot be compared. Gray and mundane, this was Conred's realm. Conred himself was solid gray, and his life force – which was very strong – was also gray. He was not original, however, and he didn't even have his own reserves of gray. He had to devour the originality of others to meet his gray needs. Gray kept him living and terribly strong. He needed large daily dosages to survive, and of course the more he had, the stronger he got.

Goodbye Self-Critical, Hello Self-Thrilled!

Just how does Conred make gray? Gray does not start out gray. Gray becomes gray through colors ignored or mashed together so they lose their brilliance. Gray itself is not original; it's not even an extreme white or black. Gray is a bland combination of faded copies of once vibrant colors from long ago. Since Conred was never able to have color of his own, he needed the colors of others to thrive. Conred would target as many potential colors from others as he could and suck in their vibrant hues. Once inside his rock-like body they would mute into gray. Not one unique color would be left.

Conred's appetite for color never ended. He was never satisfied, because he was never original. It was never enough. Being the King of Comparison, he was quite a snob about whose colors he chose to steal. He only wanted pure, undiluted colors found in the human imagination – colors that were particularly potent in children. His gray was the result of sucking the brilliant reds, yellows, greens, purples, pinks, and blues that burst forth from these young humans.

Where did Conred, King of Comparison come from? Conred comes from a world that lives in the past, a world of "already been done," a world of nothing new, a world void of vitality. Conred thrives on the vitality of humans since he has none of his own. The problem for Conred is that vitality lives in the present, but he does not. Therefore, he waits until his young targets have a big worry that causes them to focus on the past a little too long. They leave their colors hovering in space right above their little heads, and that is where Conred zaps them. He sucks their colors into himself and they become mashed and gray because they have left their original home. In turn, the children experience their first totally gray feeling – a feeling of being mundane and nothing special, of something drastically missing. When Conred steals the original colors from worrying children, he becomes strong with gray and a menacing shadow in their little lives. And the children are left to *compare for self worth, for then there will be none.*

But even boogey men have their dangers, and Conred's is the threat of the present, the Land of the New. If children stay in the Land of the New, he cannot attack. His young targets' imagination and creativity could squash Conred with new and brilliant ideas. Conred disintegrates in the Land of the New. He reigns in the Land of Worry. Conred uses the downside of logic to convince his victims – his marked ones – to stay in the Land of Worry. He loves to manipulate logic, because it, too, is created from the past. And when he manipulates logic, it creates worry about the future – a great tool for comparison. Logic is always up for grabs as to who will lead it. If Conred leads logic, it sounds something like this. Conred whispers in your ear, "They laughed at your idea, then you felt awful, so it's logical…

don't do it again, 1 + 1 = 2, conclusion: Gray!" If logic gets led by imagination, imagination might whisper, "Doesn't your idea feel good? Isn't the unknown exhilarating? Let your logic help make it happen. 1 + 1 = 2, conclusion: Color!" Conred detests imagination and the creativity that results from it. He detests the present – the Land of the New. These things keep his little marked ones untouchable by him!

In order to fight off talent and creativity, Conred had to build a strong army, and that he did. He formed two divisions of soldiers to ward off new ideas, and he devised two kinds of attack for each target. When carefully timed, these would usually keep his little victims gray for life. They would compare from the moment they woke up to the moment they went to sleep. This was the most Conred could do; sleep was never under his control because imagination was the leader there. Imagination could speak to the children in their dreams and get them to remember and see their colors. When imagination gives Conred's victims a taste of their colors, that pesky old Spirit takes charge, and before you know it, all of Conred's hard work starts to dissolve and he has lost them. Once humans have tasted their colors and had a chance to savor them again, there is no going back. Conred must make sure that while his victims are awake they are comparing all the time.

Joyce Anderson

Division #1 is titled Better Than/Less Than. The soldiers' gray uniforms have large letters displaying "less than" on the front and "better than" on the back. Then backing up Division #1 is Division #2, Not Enough/Too Much, which takes comparison to another level. Division #2 makes their victims spend time measuring how much they have, a clever waste of the precious present moment. When the children are attacked by either division, the gray uniforms come off the soldiers and are deposited into the children's' thoughts.

Conred's attack plan has three steps:

1. use a hurtful episode to keep the victims stuck in the past,
2. cause the victims to compare themselves to others, and
3. send in the soldiers to deposit their gray uniforms over the children's self worth.

This successfully disturbs all colors and originality, so that the children feel uniform. Their colors start to detach and hover above them waiting for their return to the Land of the New. Now Conred is ready to feast. Dripping and drooling, he thunders down onto the colors for a huge suck. Colors violently thrash together and the graying begins. Conred is filled with power, and his rock-hard grayness becomes so bland it is hard to look at. For a brief while Conred is satiated.

People don't seem to notice Conred because once they are grayed they rarely look up. One other oddity about Conred is that he doesn't have a back, and therefore no backbone. If you were able to see him, you would find him elevated in the air, always facing you – an immense stone-gray shape with legs and arms reaching for you. But once you "get past the past," you no longer see him if you look back.

Chapter 3

Conred and Agatha: "Who could possibly love me?"

Conred first noticed Agatha when she turned four. He was hovering over her neighborhood searching for new targets as Agatha's friends and family were celebrating her birthday. Agatha's brilliant colors were so strong they exploded over, around, and through her house. She had great strength and power to breed incredible colors through her daydreaming. She bounced through her day telling stories, which generated all kinds of colors, but especially bright pink. Conred lusted over Agatha. "Hmm," he thought, "one so colorful must be mine," and he marked her location for just the right time when he could gray her – hopefully, for life. When Conred grays someone for life, he gets every lasts delectable drop of color. He noted that Agatha would be worth waiting for, and wait he did. "After all," he recalled, "her parents were worth the wait."

Conred selects his first attack, using Divison #1, when children start school. For here is where their wild and wonderful ideas are told to step aside for training in logic. They sit in hard, gray, boxy buildings, and are told to be still and learn about the alphabet, arithmetic, history, science, and other provable topics from the past. They learn that something only has value if it can be proven, and worse, that they must constantly prove themselves and be graded. This is where they take their first steps into the world Conred has mastered. How convenient for Conred! School is a place where he can breed comparison and worry, so it's a fabulous place for one-stop shopping. Even the décor suits him. And with his comparing soldiers infiltrating their cells, Conred can keep the little darlings away from the threatening Present – far from the Land of the New. It is here at school that Conred waited for Agatha, biding his time until he could make her a devoted follower.

Agatha was beside herself to start school. She adored meeting other children, and it would be a welcome break from the current unsettling environment at home. In addition to recess, which every child loves, Agatha's favorite time during school was, of course, story time. She was thrilled to be able to learn to write and read. She couldn't wait to put her stories down on paper for others to read. After all, telling stories was what she loved to do and the gift she gave so easily. Telling stories was how Agatha shined.

Yet as the weeks went by she became frustrated. She found she could not draw the letters to look like any of the ones she saw in the books, like her teacher wrote on the chalkboard, or like her classmates had drawn. Her hands just couldn't manipulate the pencil. What was in her head would not make its way to her hands, as if her hands did not belong to her brilliant brain. She couldn't even recognize the letters herself, nor could she get them to quit moving. How could she make sense out of these letters that danced like ever-changing pick-up sticks in her head?

Soon the children caught on to this and laughed at Agatha's scribbling. By this time, many of the children had been criticized for something, so they learned to do the same to others. They humiliated Agatha, which gave her the first strong episode to compare herself with others. Conred loved watching the children's cruel words find a spot in Agatha's head where they would stay for a very long time. "You're so stupid, you can't even write," the children would taunt. The pain of their words sliced into Agatha's heart. Nothing could have been said that was more devastating to her. Her dream of writing stories, even telling them, was shattered. She was stuck in those hurtful words.

"What happened?" Agatha wondered. "School is so different from what I thought it would be."

To Agatha this building she had longed for was no more than a place to learn about uneasiness eight hours a day, five days a week. Now she yearned for the past and her happy self, not this bossy world.

"What a glorious day, she's wishing for the past!" Conred cheered in all his drooling anticipation. This was the perfect time to come after his long-awaited Agatha. Conred immediately commanded a Division #1 soldier to make the first hit. "Private Better Than/Less Than jump into Agatha's logic and carve yourself a home there. Deposit that gray uniform! Get her ready for neglect. Whisper the words that will keep her in this painful place. Let's get her ideas ready for hibernation. Agatha's ideas are very strong, so our second attack must be carefully timed."

Private Better Than/Less Than slithered into Agatha's logical brain and whispered, "They are better than you; you are less than they." He dropped his ugly uniform to slink around her brain. The uniform was the deadliest of weapons, because it was the opposite (and arch-enemy) of Original. The private's uniform and the comparison he planted in Agatha's brain created a horrible feeling in her belly, a feeling she had never known. All the padding in the world could not stop her belly from screaming at her now. "What's going on?" she wondered. She and her belly used to be such good friends long ago. Now she felt horrible, like heavy concrete. She wanted to run home and escape into her stories, but the graying had started. Her colors escaped from her unhappy body and hovered above her. "How perfect," Conred gloated, "right where I'm waiting, ready to suck!" Conred charged down onto Agatha's colors and sucked for all he was worth. As he began to drink her, screaming and crying replaced Agatha's enthusiasm to escape into her stories. She became weaker as her colorful new story ideas were shriveled by that horrible uniform of Better Than/Less Than that was now living in her head.

This new and constant use of comparison did not feel at home in her, and her body did not like it. But her logic was winning out, and as a result her body became heavy, blocked, thicker, and hard. Her heart found it harder and harder to be heard. In her head she would hear, "I am not a writer, I can't write, my stories are stupid"... on and on. Her source of color was fading. As time went on, she would try to re-create stories which would re-stir some colors, but those times were getting fewer as she let the uniform of Private Better Than/Less Than bury her stories, bury her spark, bury her colors. This would last many years.

Conred knew that a second attack would be necessary, since her colors might regenerate when she started to become a woman. Feeding off others, Conred could patiently wait for the perfect timing of his second attack so that it would be more remarkable and lasting. Private Better Than/Less Than did a good job keeping Agatha in comparison, but Conred knew that sending in his Division #2 soldier would forever seal the deal and fend off the threat of the present. Conred chose the seventh grade to make his second attack on Agatha. He savored those growing hormones and always enjoyed using them, since they were such natural tools for comparison!

With all the trouble Agatha had with reading, writing, and trying to take notes with those damned dancing letters, testing was absolutely horrible for her. But in seventh grade history class a compassionate teacher helped her each day after school. From her teacher's guidance, Agatha mustered up the strength to study in a different, but harder way than she ever did before. She wanted so badly to pass a test with a higher grade than a "D". When her teacher told stories of history Agatha could remember them, but the parts she tried to read in the textbooks never landed in her head. After pains-taking study, the day came to take the test, and to her delight she earned a "C" – a beautiful, glorious "C." Agatha was exuberant! As she received her marked test, she felt proud that she knew more than she did the weeks before. She had learned! She had actually made it into the grade range of 80%! That was even close to a "B," she was almost "Good." Conred felt Agatha's excitement and almost fainted over the smell of her colored essence starting to birth again. Thirteen and hormonal, the time was ripe. He readied Division #2 for his final attack.

This history exam happened to be an easier test than normal, and most kids got "A"s, which they gladly showed off to Agatha. Her heart sank as she watched the well-earned, beautiful "C" on her paper turn into an ugly "C" right before her eyes due to her classmates' laughter. Private Not Enough/Too Much of Division #2 entered when Agatha's heart was heavy and closed. He knew his whisper would be heard well enough. "Agatha, your 'C' is not enough," he whispered in her ear. "You are not enough, this class is too much for you, and they are all too smart." The soldier dutifully slipped off his gray uniform and placed it in a deep spot that he carved next to the uniform of Private Better Than/Less Than. Division #1 and Division #2 have now won firm ground in the war against the Land of the New. Heartbroken, Agatha suffered the loud teasing from the others about her "C." Firmly in the past and habitually comparing these heart-wrenching episodes for self worth, Agatha was now firmly in Conred's grip. Conred moaned as he started to devour her new colors that were there for such a short time.

Conred was sure that no matter what Agatha tried to do, the two uniforms that had been planted in her logical brain would dilute her talents and gifts. He was sure Agatha would be loyal. He let out a gluttonous belch as he digested into gray the last strong slurp of Agatha's favorite color, pink. Conred was done with her. He cared no more about her. He had gotten the best of Agatha.

Chapter 4

Logical Agatha

I t is true that one can get along in this world by being gray, and many do. Years went by and Agatha was informed that her learning difficulty had a name, dyslexia. She received special help and allowances for her learning differences and even attended college. She had a strong logical plan, because logic would keep her safe. Logic, which was now her guide, gave her a step-by- step list and a sense of control. Her plan was to study hard and become a registered nurse since she loved helping others. Agatha chose this career because she felt she could be safe and keep people at a distance. She could help others without bothering about her own, torn- up self. She could learn what others had to teach and not worry about her own inner world of disappointment and unrealized talent. If she kept busy helping others, surely she wouldn't have to pay attention to herself and all the hurt in her life. Others would see her as doing "good" – almost as if she would get that grade of "B" that she always revered. Her passion for her stories was deeply buried by now. After all, that was just a little girl plaything. She would not let that hurt resurface again – ever. Gray helped.

When Agatha was in college, she was walking home from the library late one night and noticed a fellow classmate following her across campus. This attention was new for Agatha. Somebody was noticing her, and her comparison words "you're not good enough" were momentarily silenced. The interested student finally approached her and asked if she would like to have coffee before she went back to her dorm. Unaccustomed to being noticed, Agatha lowered her guard and shocked herself by saying "OK." But something happened as soon as she said "OK." Her silenced, ignored, well-padded belly of years gone by decided to yell a ferocious, gut- feeling warning to her, "NOOOOO!"

This made Agatha pause, and for a split second she listened and was ready to run. But Private Better Than/Less Than, always on the attack, whispered, "Do you think you can do better? At least he notices you. Come on, settle! Go

27

with him, he's asking politely. Besides, he looks a whole lot better than you do!" Unfortunately Agatha ignored her belly and listened to the uniform that the private had installed in her logical mind. She should have listened to her belly that caused her to pause. As it turned out, this student, who was also gray, over-powered her, had his way with her body, and left her beaten up – violated and grayer than ever. This experience was a new low for Agatha, and she decided right then and there that no one would ever get in again, nor would she ever come out. And her body grew enormous with the protective padding of flesh.

Chapter 5

Coates to the Rescue

Agatha's protective padding of flesh grew to become a living guardian by the name of Coates. Coates loyally wrapped himself around her always and fiercely protected her from any feeling that had not been kind to her in the past. He understood his role clearly and simply asked for enough food to keep him around to guard her. And "around" he was – very round! For example, when a gut instinct attempted to speak to Agatha about a potential new friend approaching her, Coates pillowed it with ice cream to armor her with another ounce of flesh. "Let no one in," he would whisper, "and you can't come out either. It will only hurt". When a passion tried to spark in Agatha, Coates quickly "potato chipped" it away. After all, if it came from deep inside it couldn't be valuable outside. It could never be enough and would only lead to disappointment. When excitement tried to surface with a delicious thought,

Coates automatically squelched it with cherry pie before Agatha could really examine it. "It will only hurt" he would continually warn.

Eventually Coates became bigger, stronger, and more protective of his precious Agatha. Coates had to grow larger and larger, because all of her stored and long-ignored wishes had such potential. It was his responsibility to not let out any passion or feeling that would make Agatha vulnerable. She was not to notice them. Coates took his job seriously and prevented this from happening. As her feelings and passions got heavier, the more food Coates demanded, and the more voracious he became. For Agatha, food was one of the rare instances where something luscious from the outside world felt good going into her, a sumptuousness that she yearned for but lost long ago. Food gave her a temporary taste of the splendor of the world, even though it only lasted for seconds. Agatha believed that Coates' protection was better than being open. As one might have guessed by now, Coates is the outgrowth of the deadening uniformity of Division #1 Better Than/Less Than and Division #2 Not Enough/Too Much. He is the direct product of Conred – undeniably the cruelest of kings.

Chapter 6

Zeal: the Mundane into the Extraordinary

M uch to her credit, Agatha did graduate from college and went on to be an excellent nurse in a hospital. She even got married a few years later. Since by this time her personality signaled gray unworthiness, she attracted a gray, unworthy mate – Sid the salesman. All in all, they were a gray, unworthy couple. Sid and Agatha had each buried their unique sparkle years before they met. Their courtship began when she bought a used Ford Pinto from him. He was obviously an excellent salesman. A summarized version of their courtship went something like this:

Sid: "Hi, I'm Sid and unworthy, how about you?"

Agatha: "Yeah, I'm Agatha, but I'm sure I'm more unworthy than you."

Sid: "Cool! I need to be better than someone. Let's get married."

Agatha: "Well, I guess you're the best I can do. OK."

Sid thought that a wife would be able to handle all the mundane stuff for him while he concentrated on making as much money as he could. Love was of no interest to him. Somewhere in the background Conred chuckled as Sid and Agatha started a life of gray ever after, and Coates couldn't wait for the wedding cake.

Sid became a workaholic – not feeling enough, never satisfied with enough, and not at home enough. He did make lots of money as the world suggested. He did not want any time to be still and have to feel what was abandoned in him long ago. So Sid just kept working too much to get more and more money and admiration, but it was never enough. He saw the same thing in Agatha. She was never enough, even though by now her weight was too much, and Sid felt he had to keep reminding her of that fact. Never enough and too much equals zero, and they oddly balanced each other. This was the equation of their marriage.

As the years went by Agatha found it harder and harder to be a nurse. Caring for others while not caring for herself was taking its toll. Coates was very cumbersome to carry around and demanded much attention and feeding.

But since nurses were in demand and she was an excellent nurse, her job was secure, and so there was no need to change.

Then one day, something magical happened. Agatha felt an unusual presence in her belly. When she looked down at her massive belly she saw a glimmer of color. The more she looked, the more colors she saw, and as time went by her belly housed a sparkling rainbow. This rainbow grew larger every month until one day she birthed a colorful baby girl. Agatha named her Zeal. She tried to come up with a more acceptable name, but only the name Zeal would come out of her mouth. This rainbow child had great enthusiasm for being born, and Agatha felt immense love for this precious girl. In addition – and to her astonishment – somewhere deep beneath Coates, Agatha's own feeling of enthusiasm was stirring. A part of her she once knew was flickering again.

Sid felt Zeal's brilliance as well, but it scared him and shook him to the core – which in his case was the jingling money in his pocket. He was determined to work harder and harder to make sure there was enough for Zeal, and as a result he was home even less. Again, Sid's idea of more + less cancelled him out. This was OK with Agatha, since the more he was around, the less she felt. She did not like seeing her gray reflecting in Sid.

Zeal was fascinated with every waking and sleeping moment. Zeal's curiosity engaged her in whatever was in front of her. She was curious and fun, traits Agatha had forgotten. Zeal was color, and spread color all around. As Zeal learned to walk, talk, and grab she found her passion. What she loved to do most was quite quirky – she loved arranging. She would grab her toys, throw them in a pile, and arrange them into different settings. At various times she would organize by color, by size, by opposites, by amounts, perhaps by making them all upside down – into whatever category would grab her fancy. Then she would rearrange the same pile. She would arrange her toys, clothes, kitchen items, basement items, garage items, plants, neighbors' pets, books, and friends. Whatever she could arrange and rearrange she would. She loved making "different" out of "the same." She loved to see things in as many ways as she could. Children loved to play with Zeal, and she even started fascinating adults. Neighbors loved to see her latest arrangements, which always got people talking and imagining. These arrangements took them out of their same-old conversations and put new ideas in their minds. It brought people together and away from worries for at least a little time in their day. It was quite a strange gift for a young girl, yet her colors were strong and her arrangements were captivating. That was Zeal.

Goodbye Self-Critical, Hello Self-Thrilled!

Zeal most delighted in discovering arrangements for her mother, especially on the three 12-hour days that Agatha worked at the hospital. Agatha would pick up Zeal from her next-door neighbors' home day care center, and return home to start dinner. While Agatha was cooking, Zeal would create an arrangement that would make her Mom smile. One night while Agatha was filling the house with smells of herbs and fresh bread, Zeal had a great idea for an arrangement. She gathered costume jewelry, dresses, construction paper, books, rulers, socks, shoes, belts, and her pink ballet costume. She piled them on the living room floor. Next she gathered three lamps – a table lamp, and 2 tall floor lamps.

The table lamp she dressed as a young girl with rulers for two extended teaching arms, a pink hat made from paper, jewelry draped around her chest, and a large open mouth on the shade which she formed from a costume diamond bracelet. The glittering mouth made it look as if the girl was speaking onstage.

The first floor lamp became a nurse with a gray dress, a construction paper gray hat, and a small black straight ruler for a mouth. On the lamp's body Zeal placed an old, crinkled paper valentine that she had made the past February.

The other floor lamp became a pink flamingo. She put her pink ballet tutu made of sparkling netting around the base of the lamp. Zeal knew this flamingo was very intelligent and she displayed this by putting eyeglasses on the flamingo head she drew on the shade. She created pink flamingo wings using yard sticks as framing for an older, unraveled tutu. One wing held a storybook, and the other wing was spread wide, ready for flight. She positioned her three new friends in an arrangement as if they were talking to one another. When her arrangement was ready for view, Zeal called for her mother with a "Ready!" scream.

Agatha had been awaiting tonight's arrangement, so she stopped her cooking and ran to Zeal's newest creation. She took a look and stopped in her tracks.

Agatha had a *flash thought*– it was as if she was looking at before, during, and after pictures of her life. The small pink lamp speaking with vibrant vigor represented her when she was young. The tall gray lamp with a stiff mouth and crumpled heart felt like her today. But the flamingo, that mesmerized her. That is what she was drawn to, and a pulling in her belly urged her to come closer. This beautiful pink bird was teaching in flight with a book she knew was her writing. Zeal would usually rearrange and repeat her arrangements a total of three times before she would put her creations away. That is when Sid would come home, and to Sid this game seemed like too many messy piles around the house, which annoyed him. But tonight, without a chance to rearrange, Sid unexpectedly walked in the door early.

Zeal immediately tore her creations down. As she watched Zeal, Agatha was crushed at the destruction and could not move. To her surprise Agatha loved all three and wanted them all to remain. But it was too late; dinner was burning and Sid was grumbling. The magic moment had ended, and Agatha was heavy once again. Yet a seed had been planted.

Agatha had been waiting all night to speak with Zeal, so when she put her to bed she asked, "Zeal, how did you come up with those lamp arrangements?"

Zeal thought about this for a long time, since she had never before considered the question "how." "Hmmm…I close my eyes and watch my imagination, and when I see what I like, I choose it, play with it, and it just happens."

"Zeal, those lamps were me," Agatha whispered, "when I was a little girl, how I am now, and how I really hope I could be very soon. But, how do you know so much about me? How did I get into your head like that?"

"Mommy, it's not in my head. My head feels too small to hold everything out there," she says as she points above and all around her. "So I go to my heart. That's the biggest place I know, and that's where it comes from. I just play with what I love, I get lots of ideas, and I arrange the one I love the most. Tonight I was imagining when you were a little girl, and that's what came to me."

Agatha teared up as she looked at her lovely little girl and said, "Zeal, you must always, always do this. Never put it away." Agatha remembered the sting of doing just that. Agatha kissed Zeal all over her neck and head, tickling her until she giggled and said good night.

The colors emanating from Zeal's bedroom on this particular night were doubly strong and blew forcefully though the roof. Conred stopped short in his regular nightly scanning for victims, and like a magnet, he was drawn to Zeal's home. "Yum! I've tasted this intense combination of colors before," he remembered, since memory is his strong suit. "This child moves to the top of my list," he resolved, and followed her closely from that moment on.

Chapter 7

Zeal's Pause

As Zeal began her fifth year, she started to notice something peculiar. She had the gift of seeing colors and something smoky-looking in people. She could see that many people did not let their colors out, so they looked stuck. They hoarded their colors inside gray borders. This made Zeal sad, especially when she viewed it in her loving mother and even in Sid. Many times she would notice the colors start to vibrate in her mother when they played together. She hoped they would burst through her mother's gray borders, and sometimes they did, even if only for a brief moment. But it rarely lasted, and gray would cover the color once again. Then Zeal started noticing it in some of the older neighborhood children. She contemplated this puzzle deeply, which caused her to slow down. This dilemma gave her pause.

Agatha began to notice Zeal was arranging less and less, and that her zest was slowing down. This disturbed Agatha tremendously and she wanted to snap Zeal out of it. She missed her daughter's arrangements. And there was something else about Zeal's pause that haunted Agatha. Zeal had ignited something deep inside Agatha. She felt a deep connection in her heart to what was worrying Zeal, and even though she didn't really know what it was, she knew she had to help her daughter. And suddenly, a strong flash thought came to Agatha – do something different! Agatha's instant thought (which seemed to have come from nowhere) was to take Zeal to work with her at the hospital. Zeal could visit the children's ward while Agatha worked. Zeal was immediately on board for this excursion!

When Zeal walked into the children's ward, she was enraptured. The room was vivid with color – filled with clowns, animals, balloons, and carousels painted on the walls, ceiling, and floor. She looked up to see a painted sky with sun, moon, planets, and stars. To add to this fantasy-filled room, the children all wore their favorite pajamas – cowboys, ballerinas, super heroes, and many more characters played with each other, even stuck in their small hospital beds. There were stuffed animals all around the room and the children's artwork was everywhere. Tables and shelves housed crayons, paints, hats, colored construction paper, glue, scissors, colorful books, blackboards, and etch-a- sketches. It was the most rainbow place Zeal had ever been. She had seen vibrant colors before, but none with the intensity she found in this ward. The robust rainbows she saw in these children matched her own. The children's artistry caressed them, so that even in bodily illness, they were thriving.

Exploding with color, Zeal had zest again. Her arranging hands were alive and didn't know where to begin. So many choices! So she just touched the first item she saw (a pile of paint brushes), and she was on her way. As she was arranging with these children, she paid no attention to their illnesses, only their colors. Best of all, they also saw it in her. There's nothing like playing with your peers. Zeal had no concept of how much time had passed until she noticed something quite bewildering. When the adults entered the ward with their boarded- up rainbows, their gray would dissolve, and their released rainbows would shoot out like fireworks. Yet as the adults left the room, their gray started to slowly vacuum their rainbows back and tuck them away. What was so horrible out there, she wondered, to cost them their colors? Zeal looked at the clock and noticed that Agatha would arrive soon to take her home. Zeal felt wonderful here and did not want to leave the rainbows. She wondered if the gray would also seep into her if she left this room. Zeal decided then and there that she was not going to leave this ward.

Agatha finished her shift and went to the children's ward to pick up Zeal. Running to Agatha to wrap her in a hug, Zeal said, "Oh Mommy, what a wonderful place. I love it here."

"I knew you would," Agatha answered. "I want you to tell me all about it on the way home. But now grab your coat and let's say goodbye."

"But Mommy, I am staying here. Look how colorful everyone is. Mommy, look at your rainbow!" Just as Zeal's words sailed in the air, Agatha felt "tickled pink." She looked down at her body and, sure enough, she saw her long-missing rainbow outlined in pink from deep inside her. It spiraled up through Coates, who was bewildered at its return.

Agatha had realized several months ago why she named her daughter Zeal. Her daughter saw the zeal in everyone and she ignited it when her eyes gazed at theirs. And Agatha was no exception. "Oh, Mommy, look at your colors, especially that sparkly pink color all around you!" Agatha was speechless, and once again felt "tickled pink."

She did indeed feel her long lost colors, including her favorite pink which was making a special appearance. She had never felt that shade so dazzling before.

Coates was alarmed at this discovery, and started grumbling ferociously around Agatha's belly. He was freaking out at the possibility that Agatha would be vulnerable, and worse yet, that he could be ignored! Coates repeated his alarming grumble until he finally got Agatha's attention. "Zeal, we must go home for dinner," Agatha said suddenly. "Let's leave so the children can get some rest and heal." Agatha grabbed Zeal's resisting hand and they started to leave the room.

Just then, Agatha's strong, but long-padded instinct was stirred awake through her moment of color. This made her body take pause. She stopped in her tracks. She felt danger. Her belly got through to her and signaled, "Leave Zeal here! Go to the window!"

Agatha dropped Zeal's hand as she felt pulled to the window. She looked out, down, around, and finally up. And that is when she saw Conred, larger than ever, looming over the children's ward, salivating over the hues he planned to engulf. Agatha knew Zeal was his next target. Perplexed, Agatha wondered why today, of all days, she discovered Conred. Why had she not noticed him before? Deep down, Agatha realized that Conred had been around for years. "He is such a horrible, dead feeling," she thought. And feel him she did! "This feeling is worse than any fear I have given to Coates," Agatha decided.

Conred was not very happy as he spun above the hospital in a reeling rage. How did Zeal end up at the children's ward? That was the last place he wanted her to be. But ohhhh, the colors there today were exceptionally blinding, seductive, and hard to resist. He had always tried to stay away from the children's hospital, seductive as it was, because of the children's comfort in the present and their camaraderie. Plus, there were all those damn nurses helping the children feel OK the way they were. Yuck! Their joy was no match for his artillery of worry. "*&*%@#!! Why is my Zeal in there?" Conred cursed. "I want her out!" For the first time ever, Conred considered whether or not he should wrestle with the nurses to get Zeal. And his soldiers, as always, were standing by to do his bidding.

Conred was worried that Zeal would be too dangerous a threat to let her grow any older without graying. Her colors would grow too strong to capture. Her colors could take the worry out of any situation, and that would make

50

Conred's power flat and void. Conred knew that he had met his match in Zeal. She could see colors in everything, even the gray. "Zeal could undo all my hard work," Conred barked. "She could release the rainbows from everyone I've grayed, and then where would I be? I would be nothing, dissolved!" Conred sensed his possible demise, and with steel in his voice he commanded his soldiers, "We will not wait until she begins school. We must gray Zeal! Let us make a plan!"

But even with the risk he felt, Conred was seduced by Zeal. He would not relinquish the dream of his greatest conquest – the taste of Zeal. She would be the most delectable feast he had ever experienced. He knew her colors would be better than any he digested. Her creativity would be the hardest to break, but his reward would be the juiciest.

Meanwhile, Agatha decided intuitively that it was best to leave Zeal in the children's ward for the night. She made a bed for her daughter that was protected by the colors of the children. Agatha knew Zeal would be safe in the children's ward. She tucked her in, hugged her tightly, kissed her goodnight, and lovingly whispered, "I will see you in the morning."

Chapter 8

Tellaga

As she left the hospital and looked at Conred hovering above, Agatha wondered how she could have been so unaware of him until today. What had happened? Somehow Agatha knew that he had been around for years. But today, she knew his name, could see him, and was acutely aware of his deadening power. As Agatha drove home, frantic over what to do, she heard Private Better Than/Less Than start to work on her, "See, Zeal is better off there than with you. Look how happy she was. She did not want to leave. She does not need you." Private Too Much/Not Enough doubled-dipped her with "Zeal's rainbow is too much for you; you are not enough to be with her colors."

Too many years of living with the uniformity of those soldiers had made it easy to give in to them. Agatha needed an answer on how to save Zeal. But by the time she got home, she was in tears, fraught with despair, and void of creativity. No Zeal! Coates was burning a hole in Agatha's gut and nagging her to get something into her that felt good. Instant gratification was the key for Coates to keep thriving, and this was another habit that Agatha let take over.

As she barged through the front door, Agatha hurriedly went to the kitchen and flung herself at the refrigerator for some instant nurturing. But something was different. It was that color pink that Zeal had noticed and was now showing up for her own view. Something powerful was stirring inside Agatha, more powerful than Conred or Coates. Inside her body, she felt a fight beginning. Her body started contorting in odd shapes, small at first and then growing, thrusting her around the kitchen. She could sense that Conred's soldiers were warring against something new and threatening to them. They were fighting to hold onto their Agatha. Something was shaking them up, causing them to lose their positions. And as they were flailing to find new ground, Agatha grabbed the refrigerator door to steady herself. She wrapped her arms around the refrigerator and held on tightly as the war inside her was escalating. She felt like she was being torn up inside from the battle and from missing her precious Zeal. Agatha sobbed, realizing that she was once again at the refrigerator, her constant refuge whenever she was troubled. Stuffing the emptiness of her pain at the refrigerator was the reason Agatha was able to get through all those painful years. But this time…this time she craved a different reason. As her frustration changed to fury, Agatha tried to throw the refrigerator over and screamed, "No more, you have never helped!"

At that instant, as all that emotion escaped from her gut, Agatha felt the refrigerator change form within her arms. The cold metal started to soften into a tickling, fizzy, gentle pressure. It felt warm, tingling, and magnetic – as if she was holding onto an enormous sparkle. Agatha released her arms and stepped back to view what had just happened. She could not believe her eyes, and to be sure her eyes were very big! Where the refrigerator once stood, was a sparkling, soft pink form with the hint of a lioness mane around a human female shape, as if it was made of glittered cotton candy. She was floating between Agatha's cabinets where the refrigerator had been. The pink woman had a beautiful sateen face and a swooped-back, pink dreadlocked mane that was covered with diamonds. Agatha couldn't take her eyes off the beautiful pink creature, who spoke in a musical voice with a firm resonance that made Agatha tremble. "Agatha," she said, "what is your different reason?"

Stunned and completely confused, Agatha tries to put together words to form an answer. "Who… what hap-… how did…where…Who are you?"

"I am Tellaga."

"What are you?" Agatha pleads.

"You will find out soon enough, and I promise we are going to save Zeal. But let's start with first things first. I have come to the place where you can view me because you have declared a true and **different reason** for wanting me."

"Wanting you? I don't know who or what you are."

"Agatha, you must get relaxed in order to hear what you are about to hear. Please, start with a deep breath," Tellaga orders. Agatha does as she is told, since she is used to obeying without question. "Again, breathe deeply." Tellaga has her repeat this a few more times. "Now drop your head and gaze into your heart…breathe into your heart…close your eyes." This is all new to Agatha, but it seems perfectly natural to do what Tellaga suggests. And strangely enough, just being with this beautiful, pink creature gives Agatha a hint of relief. She starts to trust Tellaga, whoever she is.

"Next, wrap your arms around your belly."

Whoops! This is where Tellaga loses her. Agatha tightens up, takes a stand, and replies, "Are you kidding? I can't reach around my belly, and I certainly will not hug that part of me!" Agatha is adamant. As a matter of fact, she hasn't been that adamant for as long as she can remember, and that feels strong. She senses a color of red coming through and feels a bit sturdier.

Tellaga tries another approach, "Okay, then close your eyes and just imagine connecting your heart to your belly, over and over again." This suggestion works, since Agatha gets to close her eyes and doesn't have to touch her belly in front of Tellaga. "Keep blending your heart and belly," Tellaga encourages. A minute later, Agatha opens up and starts to feel room inside.

Tellaga continues, "Agatha, when you were clutching the refrigerator earlier, you were aware of a different reason for wanting me. What was that different reason?"

"Did I want you? I don't know what you mean!"

"Yes."

Unaware, Agatha hugs her belly as she starts to think about this. She notices currents stirring within her, a crackling feeling coming to the surface. A rumbling begins in her tummy and grows increasingly louder. Spiraling colors appear and make their way to her heart to gather fuel. The spiral then jets its way up her body and lands in a sea of blue in her beautiful throat.

And for the first time in years, Agatha allows her mouth to open for her deep insides to speak. The locked-up words are dying to get out after all these years, and explode from her mouth as she delivers her different reason. "I WANT ZEAL BACK!"

Tellaga looks at her, more stunning than ever, and takes a step closer to Agatha.

Agatha examines her explosion and thinks, "but of course, I want my daughter back."

Tellaga tells her, "There is more. Again tell me your reason."

Tears of color stream down Agatha's face as she suddenly understands that it is not only her daughter she is talking about. With calm confidence and clarity she says, "I want my zeal back."

"Yes," Tellaga replies.

Tellaga takes one more step closer and Agatha feels her warmth.

Agatha looks longingly into Tellaga's eyes and says, "I want Agatha back."

Tellaga says, "Yes," and lets Agatha sit with this truth. Tellaga offers, "She has never left. Coates hid her to protect you from hurt, yet the price for this protection has numbed your life. It has cost you your stories." Agatha knows this is true. Tellaga continues, "I am your zeal…I am You." Agatha gasps deeply as this truth fills her up.

"I live in the World of Vitality where there is no talent better than another, no comparison. There is just encouragement and limitless ideas for what you love to be used and shared. I steer you to where you match up in the world, where you are desired." Agatha is hanging on to every word.

"But when you feel you are losing me, when you feel you can't find me, then you are living the exact opposite of me. Come back to me by imagining the exact opposite of Conred."

"What do you mean? What do you know of Conred?" Agatha asks.

"He is everywhere. He helps us learn what we don't want. He actually bores us in the World of Vitality. Now back to the rule of opposites. Here are a lot of examples: "I use what you love; Conred does not. I am deep within you; Conred is outside. My presence feels freely flowing in your whole body; Conred feels heavy and tight, especially in your head. I am always here now; Conred ignores now. I like the unknown; Conred only works with what has already happened – where is the creativity in that? I love; Conred fears. Shall I go on?" Agatha clearly says, "No, I see."

Chapter 9

Extra-ordinary Agatha

T ellaga knows it is time to dig out all the experiences of Agatha and quilt them together into a beautiful masterpiece. Agatha will be the artist; her brush will be Tellaga, her intuition. "Let's go back to what you loved and buried. When you were four and five years old, do you remember telling stories without any preparation? Do you remember how you couldn't wait to give them away?"

Agatha allows herself to remember those sweet times when she made stories for her mother and her friends, when she felt excited about each day. She remembers the time when she didn't feel "Less Than," when she simply felt ENOUGH: "Yes," she says, her voice full of emotion.

"When you told your stories, you ignited your listeners' curiosity. You awakened their eagerness for "what's next." Well, dear Agatha, that is your IT, the extra-ordinary you. Your stories encourage people to trust the unknown. And when people are comfortable in the unknown, they are free to create and use their IT. Your stories showed them not to worry about the results – the results will gladly follow their IT."

"But Tellaga, there is so much out there that has hurt me, and I don't know where it will come from next. How can I tell stories of the unknown when I'm so afraid after all that has happened to me?"

"Because now you remember me, and I cannot go away. I will guide you IN TU IT. Here's how I will help. If a person comes up to you with an idea that might smother your fabulous IT, I will make your body feel like concrete. I will signal you with an emphatic NO, especially in your belly."

As Agatha hears this, Conred flashes into her mind. That is what she has been feeling for years. He has been there for years, that concrete blob!

"By the same token, if someone comes up to you with an idea that ignites your IT, I will signal your body with a YES. It will feel open, alive, and flowing, like there is a party inside you. And I will instantly lead you IN TU IT."

Agatha remembers exactly what that feels like, before she started living in hurt, before there was Coates and her body was separate from IT. She remembers playing, hugging, and telling her stories, with no separation from her body or her heart. She felt wonderful before she had to take care of Coates.

Tellaga continues, "And Agatha there will be many times when I won't signal either way. You'll get an idea, meet someone, or see or hear something, and it might get your attention, but my signals might not come to you yet. This is very important as well, because it means DO NOTHING YET. Be still, be silent, be patient, and be aware – don't ignore my "no-sign". Doing nothing is doing something. Things are happening that you can't see. Other people's ITs are involved and you must patiently wait for them to join you. Then I will signal you clearly."

Agatha says, "I'm used to doing nothing about me, so that should be easy."

Tellaga immediately interrupts her and says, "No, you have been doing something all these years. You have been ignoring me and feeding Coates. That is something! Paying attention to my signal of DO NOTHING YET means that you are aware of me and you don't hide. You know my YES or NO signal will come at the perfect time. You TRUST – that's the difference."

Tellaga sparkles as she explains further, "Now comes the best part. When I signal you with YES, it means you are connecting with others' ITs and their YESes. You won't know about that yet or how it will turn out. The result is not yours to know. But I will know, as will other people's

"Tellagas." That's the best part of the unknown. That's where your YES signals to others who will be working with their YESes, using their ITs. When everyone works with their IT, life is full. It's magic! It's synchronicity."

Agatha takes in all of this. She remembers when she was telling her stories, she didn't care about what was going to happen after them, just that she could tell them and be with others. She loved the unknown then, and she created so easily from that place. She looks at Tellaga and asks, "So all I have to do is feel a YES, NO, or DO NOTHING YET in my body?"

"That's all you have to do."

"I'm so afraid of getting hurt again."

"Agatha, your stories are there whether you are afraid or not. Everyone's IT is there whether they are afraid or not. Whether you use your IT or not depends on moving away from worry and from your past. Then pay attention to me, I am your all-ways."

"Don't you think I want to do that?" Agatha cries. "I hate worrying. But how do I move worry out of the way?" In this very moment of worry, Tellaga sees the uniforms of Private Better Than/Less Than and Private Not Enough/ Too Much start to pull at Agatha. They try to stuff Agatha's pink into their gray sleeves and pants, but they can't hold onto this pink – it is too effervescent. Tellaga says, "I see the bland uniforms of Conred's soldiers inside you. I know

Conred has been in you for quite some time. That coward
loves to attack unsuspecting first graders. Agatha, aren't
you tired and, most of all, bored with Conred yet?"

Agatha looks at her curiously, and Tellaga says louder,
"Aren't you bored with him yet? Boredom is a great
motivator."

"Well, I never quite thought of it that way… but…"
and rage starts frothing forward in solid, purposeful
black. It is not a bland gray any longer. It builds and
builds until Agatha explodes, "I'm sick and tired of him!
I'm smothering! I'm so confused. I help people every day
at work. I'm a good mother to Zeal and a dutiful wife. I'm
capable of all these things, and I do so much. Why do I
feel so dull? Why am I so huge?!! I even went to college
and studied so hard when I could barely read and write.
And, and…and…" Tears well up in Agatha's eyes once
again. "That horrible boy…I was raped, raped, raped!"
Now the flood gates are opened. "I was raped by him –
raped of my stories, raped of writing and reading, raped
of my happy parents, raped of me!" Agatha is unable to
stop the tears, and loses control, falling to the floor.

She shakes the house, she is sobbing so hard. She is
shaking to her core. And as all those hurtful thoughts and
feelings pour out of Agatha, there is now room inside her
for Tellaga to come home. Agatha looks at Tellaga with
longing, and then closes her eyes. Tellaga steps closer and

moves into Agatha. Agatha gasps deeply as she senses Tellaga filling her, anchoring in her heart. She hugs her belly as she feels Tellaga stretch out into every finger, every toe, and every cell.

As Agatha and Tellaga merge, the layers of feelings that Coates had padded for years begin deflating. Coates suddenly feels weak, and thinking that he still has to protect his Agatha, he pulls out the heavy artillery. He puts images of key lime pie, gooey cheeseburgers, chips and dip, pizza, and macaroni and cheese in Agatha's mind. But those images pale in comparison to this new feeling of release. Coates even tries to distract Agatha with images of healthy food that she can stuff herself with. But alas, she has no urgency in her, no reaching outside for help. Coates notices something inside her that is replacing him – something else that is feeding and nurturing her, and he knows that very soon, he will no longer be fed by Agatha.

"Let's dissolve Conred and Coates for good, shall we?" Tellaga offers. And Agatha notices that Tellaga's voice is now speaking to her from the inside, from within her mind, from her intuition. "In order for them not to bother you," Tellaga continues, "you must befriend them."

"Whoa, Whoa, Whoooaaaa!" Agatha rebels. "Why on earth should I do that?"

"Because friends don't attack friends, and they have taught you how not being you just does not work. They provided lessons. Now it's time to neutralize them and let them go. Let's start with Coates. Thank Coates for being there for you all those years."

"That's a stretch. Are you kidding?"

"Agatha, you just wanted to feel better, and Coates did that for you in a delicious-tasting instant. You didn't know what else to do with your hurt. Coates gave you something from the outside that tasted good in you for a split second. It was the best he could do and the best you could do clouded in hurt. He was helping you feel some pleasure when you were so down, keeping your mind off feelings. Thank him for being there until you were ready for me. But now you have to let him go."

Agatha looks at the layers on her arms, her legs, her belly, her hands, and tiredly, from all her years of hating Coates, she simply gives in and says, "Thank you." At that moment she feels how full she is with Tellaga. Agatha cannot believe how she has no more concerns about Coates in any way. Somehow he is no longer a part of her worries. She notices a tingling in her body as she feels Coates begin the job of dissolving.

Tellaga continues, "Coates was an offshoot of Conred. Shall we deal with him now?"

"Yes, we must get to Zeal!" Agatha urgently pleads.

"And now you have *your* zeal to do just that!

Are you ready to befriend Conred?"

"You are really going to have to help me with that one. When I think of him, I think of a keyless prison, and my throat and mouth go dead. How can I befriend him?"

"Agatha, he is the simplest one to understand. Conred is tied into our main lesson as human beings. Being human is about experiencing the ***imagined*** absence of love – such as how much you realize you love something once it's gone or what comes up when you can't be you. You imagine you're not good enough, loveable enough, talented enough, or smart enough. You imagine you have to be more and that you will be graded on what you do. You imagine there is someone better than you at what you love to do. Jealousy comes in then, and you don't feel special enough. You imagine you must be the one and only person to do something wonderful in order to get noticed, to get love. This is what Conred teaches. And in this way he leads you to the highest, because in the full you, there is room for everyone to be wonderful. No talent is better than another – it's all appreciated, it's all needed. Your love for IT is never gone; you just imagine that it is. How fabulous when life brings you back to that realization. It was all just imagined."

Agatha begins to understand her relationship with Conred.

Tellaga continues, "When we imagine there is no love, we stifle who we really are. We war, we fear, we hoard, we hurt, we disconnect. We hate missing love. The human challenge is in realizing that love has always been there, deep inside all of us. We pull the shade down over it when we feel hurt. But life is about pulling the shade back up by learning from the hurt."

"Let's do the math, as they say." Tellaga urges. "It's really quite a good subject to learn from. Let's review multiplication."

Agatha rolls her eyes, "That's OK, really, we don't have to go there. I get it."

Tellaga ignores Agatha and plunges ahead. "Here are the three equations we will work with:

a positive x a positive = a positive

a positive x a negative = a negative

a negative x a negative = a positive

Let's plug you into Equation 1. What have you learned today that adds to your IT?"

"I loved making up stories and telling them," Agatha answers.

"Good. Equation 1: creating stories multiplied by sharing stories equals extraordinary you. A positive times a positive equals a positive. Now, plug in a negative about loving to tell your stories for the second equation."

Agatha knows exactly what her first negative was. "Not getting to tell my stories because I wasn't enough, and school was too much. The other kids were better than me in class work and made fun of me. I couldn't write or read like the others. Conred showed me that!"

"Yes, he is very clever," Tellaga agrees. "So Equation 2: loving to tell your stories multiplied by believing you're stupid equals you stopping doing what you love. A positive times a negative is a negative. How did that work for you?"

"I've felt dull every since," Agatha admits.

"Now let's look at Equation 3. All negatives can turn into a positive. So hiding your stories and comparing for self worth are two negatives."

Confused, Agatha asks, "How do they become a positive?"

"When you Go to the Learning! Learning is found in the present. What have your two empty negatives taught you?"

"That I always listened to Conred. I hid what I loved, so I wouldn't be noticed. I didn't want to be hurt or laughed at anymore. Conred was my Geiger counter. I used him to figure out where I fit in. I wanted Coates to help me not to feel, but I did feel. I felt empty, and I suppose I was easy to push around. It was easy for others to do what *they* wanted to do with me. Even after having my beloved Zeal, the emptiness was always in the corner. Tellaga, I have learned that hiding what I love about me has hurt me more than what anybody out there could possibly say or do."

"Good, Agatha! Do you feel negative at this moment?"

"No, I feel good...I feel relief...I feel discovered!"

"That's because you are in the moment and the learning, and you have let go of the past.

Who did that?"

"I did, I did!" Agatha sighs.

"The equations are about you – when you're not you, and when you are. It is the "Ah Ha! Moment" when your negatives teach you the positive. But it's up to you to DO THE MATH."

Agatha feels full. In fact, she starts to feel like Tellaga looks. Pink sparkles tingle her skin, and an aurora of diamonds surrounds her, pouring out from her belly – that lovely companionship of heart and belly that she now realizes is Tellaga. Then, Agatha instantly has a special "Ah Ha! Moment." She knows the meaning of the name

Tellaga – to Tell Aga of her story. She loves her new name.

"By the way, Agatha, this is how you will de- gray and handle Conred."

Chapter 10

Conred Ready

T he mention of Conred brings her back to what she must do – retrieve Zeal. Taking on the name of Tellaga, she gets in her car with no plan, just the faith of her belly guiding her. As she drives to the hospital, she wonders how she will confront Conred. The word "story" flashes into her mind for a split second, and she feels her body signal strength to her. She has learned that her body with tell her YES, NO, or DO NOTHING YET on any idea she has. YES to "story" signals her now. She feels open in her heart, her eyes are a little livelier, and the excitement of creativity starts to brew in her body.

She is surprised that doing what she loves is going to help her get Zeal. Just imagine: being in Conred's company and telling him a story is what is going to get Zeal back. There is no denying this. She realizes she still feels scared, but now she also feels armed. It's been so long since she's told a story, and she feels that her skills are beyond rusty. How on earth will she get him to listen when he is hell-bent on drinking the colors of Zeal and maybe the other children as well?

As she nears the hospital, she sees the cloud of Conred hovering over it. His soldiers are by his side. Tellaga is no longer shaken by the sight of them. She can see how rote they are. They do the same thing over and over, every day. Private Better Than/Less Than and Private Not Enough/ Too Much are so predictable. They don't think for themselves; they are slaves to Conred. Their gray is so dull that Tellaga yawns. "What a snooze they are!" Tellaga thinks. "How could I listen to them every day since I was a child and not get rid of them from sheer boredom?" This amuses her and she is surprised by her chuckle in the middle of all of this.

Tellaga walks closer and closer to Conred, strength growing in her with every step. She decides to make eye contact with Conred, and she does not let go. Conred looks at her in disbelief, shaken by her boldness. She is getting to him and they both know it. She will not look away. Conred is astounded. No one has ever had the nerve to find him and look at him directly. He becomes curious at what she is seeing in him and wonders whether he looks frightening enough. "Enough," that awful word, is creeping into Conred's own thoughts now. As Tellaga feels the charge running through her, she slowly creates a beautiful, intentional smile just for Conred. Then she tops it off with a seductive wink.

This infuriates Conred. "What a fat fool! How dare you look directly at me!" he roars indignantly. Enraged, he unwraps his arms from his humped, rock body and flails them up and down with such force that he accidentally knocks his soldiers' hard, dull heads together. As Private Better Than/Less Than collides into Private Not Enough/Too Much there is a tremendous, cracking thunder as their bodies dismantle into crumbling pebbles that fall below into the luscious green grass. Conred is so disgruntled and distracted with Tellaga that he is unaware of the demise of his soldiers. Little does he know that their uniforms have already made a home inside his own thoughts. "How dare someone look at me! Where are those bumbling soldiers of mine? This Fat Agatha needs an extra dose of gray," he bellows, secretly suspecting that her uniforms are quickly being colored into original costumes. "Fat, Obese, Stupid, No- Talent Woman," he screams at her, deciding he has to do some of his own gray work. "Who do you think you are, staring at a king – especially Conred, The Great King of Comparison?"

Tellaga holds her stare and sees Conred's words come out of his mouth like flat, dark pick-up sticks. For the first time, she is actually glad she has dyslexia. As the jumbled letters of Conred's hurtful words shoot towards her, she sends them a burst of pink fizz. The detached letters are no match for the power of her pink, and they breeze through her harmlessly and out the other way. Tellaga is amazed at the weakness of these words that used to freeze her dead. She feels such calm and grace. With her gaze locked on Conred, she smiles, lifts her soft, puffy hand, and curls her right index finger towards him, urging him to come closer, closer, and closer still.

Conred's anger is beyond compare. "Where is her calm coming from?" he wonders. "How can a king as great as I not shake her up?" Then he has a sudden, troubling thought: "maybe there is a king *better than* me!" He quickly catches himself and notices what he is doing. "I have to get hold of myself and control this situation. I must shake this fat woman!" And then Conred remembers the reason she is here: she is lacking her precious Zeal! Conred's desire for this child surpasses everything, even the memory of his desire for the colors of the young Agatha. But his drive to gray Zeal has him worried now, since his soldiers are missing. How can he get Zeal without them? A small crack appears in Conred's rock body as he realizes his soldiers are gone. "I've got to replace them and fast!" He tries to remember when and where he first employed them, but is interrupted again by that large, annoying woman. As he looks down to deal with Tellaga, he notices a pink sparkly fizz outlining her.

"Oh, Connnnred" she calls with a singsong tone. "I have some colors I want to offer you. I just want to give them to you; you don't even have to steal them. Don't fret about your soldiers. Just come down here and sit with me while I tell you a story."

Conred is feeling weaker and weaker. "That damn fat woman is right," Conred thinks to himself. "I do need some colors to bland. Where are those idiotic soldiers? I need my daily dose." He contemplates Tellaga's offer. "It would be helpful to suck some colors without figuring out how to steal them on my own. I need all my strength for little Zeal. I'll outfox this annoying woman. I'm too much for her to be a threat to me. My soldiers have already done their work on her years ago, so why not suck a little of that pink? There is certainly plenty to have – she's got 'weigh' too much!" he chuckles at his own joke.

But Conred hates to be close to his targets, so he only lowers a little towards Tellaga. He must get the upper hand. He ponders how he can grab the colors without his soldiers, since they spread so far and wide. Conred is suspicious of Tellaga's generosity and wonders how she plans to just give him some pink. But he is sure that her gray uniforms are still hidden somewhere deep in her fat and he can activate them. "Hey, Largest Lard Ass in Town with an Ass's IQ to match," he calls out to Tellaga. "I've always wondered how Sid even got close enough to you to give you a baby." He laughs. "It seems physically impossible that Sid could even survive the mating."

By this time a huge crowd has formed and they are flabbergasted at what they are witnessing. Tellaga senses her daughter and looks up to see Zeal peering out the window of the children's ward. Conred and Tellaga's banter is being heard throughout the attentive silent town.

Tellaga takes a deep breath and again dissolves Conred's hateful words into dyslexic letters that fall away. She refuses to let them get stuck inside her. This helps her see even more fizzy pink, and she is stirred as a story begins to form. Holding her gaze on Conred, she beckons him over with her finger for a second time.

Conred is getting his second wind. He feels his power growing as he notices the crowd. Surely an audience this large is only suited for a king as great as he is. But he is still annoyed that Tellaga continues to call him towards her. He decides he will do his greatest work in front of everyone. For more artillery, he plunges into his strong memory and recalls how he first grayed her. "Hey Agatha," he calls out, using her old name, "remember those stupid stories you used to tell that everyone made fun of? They made no sense, and you bored everyone. You couldn't even write them down for others to read. That should have been your sign from the so-called "universe" for you to shut up and bless us all with your silence! What a no-talent, worthless, no-reason-to-be- alive idiot you were! People couldn't stand you! And now you think you have a story to tell me, the greatest audience of all?"

Tellaga gasps as the full force of Conred's words hit her. She is in disbelief. Her eyes widen, her mouth drops. She slowly lifts her body to stand tall, looks at her daughter, the people- filled windows in the surrounding buildings, and moves her gaze downward to view the increasing audience surrounding her, waiting for her response. She looks slowly into Conred's eyes. Tellaga has her epiphany. Those words that flew out of Conred's mouth to embarrass and belittle her – those exact letters placed in perfect order to form the words she had tried to avoid hearing her whole life – those words were now in front of her for all to hear, judge, and compare. Her worst fear has now been realized in the greatest possible way.

In amazing relief, Tellaga wonders, "Is that all there is? Those words I've spent my whole life keeping others from saying, building layers and layers of protective blubber, and that was all there is – blubbering, blubbering words?" She is amused and starts to laugh at herself, and she realizes that this limited alphabet is in everyone. Letters and words can never describe the whole of anything. She now loves the wisdom of her dyslexia even more, dyslexia that pushes and touches greater knowledge. Words are inadequate at saying it all, but the one place she can find the whole of everything and everyone is in the heart. And in an instant Tellaga knows grace – grace for herself and grace for all.

She realizes the beauty of her gift of story, to use our shared letters in a way that takes each person to their limitless heart and imagination – a place where everyone is enough, no one is little, and there is no comparing. Here we find ourselves and know our worth. Here we discover our purpose.

With this new found grace, Tellaga decides to dyslexify Conred's words. With his words still hovering in the air, Tellaga opens her massive arms, gathers the mixed-up letters, disarms the words, and pulls them gracefully into her chest, deeply into her heart. The letters have become red hot fire in her chest, and she feels the passion of them. She bears it, welcoming the color red. Alchemy! She knows compassion. She knows Conred. The story brewing within her for Conred is complete and she is ready to share it.

Joyce Anderson

81

Chapter 11

Conred's Story

As the story comes through, Agatha has the urge to circle where she is standing. With her arms outstretched like a flamingo, she circles and dances. This makes Conred dizzy as he watches her. She moves more and more. She sees the people all around her with grays covering their color, and she loves them so. She sees what Zeal has always seen. Everyone has color at their core. She walks closer to Conred, and as she does, a layer of blubber melts off. She feels lighter. She takes another step closer and another layer melts away, since she has no more need of it. By the time she steps close to Conred, the last layer has left her body. The true Tellaga is revealed, and she is stunning!

The crowd is aghast. Zeal and the children are not surprised and filled with joy. On the other hand, Conred is furious. He knows that the uniforms stored in her head are gone. He has no idea how to attack her, since she is not storing the past anymore. He does not know how to gray without it. Her calm unnerves him. He feels heat in his rock eyes, burning as he stares at her. Tellaga squints as she thinks she sees red in his eyes – fiery red, with hits of orange and yellow. "Whoa! A color in Conred?" she muses. She smiles, sure now of his story.

The burning in Conred makes his eyes moist. "Where does this moisture come from? I am solid!" he tells himself hatefully. To get Conred to sit near her, Tellaga envisions the color red, which actually surrounds them. She knows this is the color wanting to surface in Conred. The red in him is drawn to her, so it moves him closer. He cannot hold himself back, and he reluctantly sits near her.

"Conred, your story is fascinating," Tellaga says admiringly. "Wouldn't you like to hear it?" Conred's favorite subject is himself, of course, and his reserves of confidence are running rather low. This, he decides, must be why he is willing to sit next to her. "Yes, Agatha, I would enjoy watching you make a fool of yourself trying to tell a story, even with the most fascinating subject there is – a king as great as I. Please, by all means, begin," he snickers.

"Ah, red!" Tellaga begins. "It is a beautiful color. It's a color we feel warm and alive in. Wouldn't you agree? And it comes from a most interesting land, where everything is red, as far as the eye can see. Thanks to orange and yellow, there are many shades of red in this land. Can you imagine this place, Conred? The trees, flowers, rivers, mountains, rain, and sunshine are all red – from deep crimsons and scarlets to the palest hues and tints. Even the people, Conred, were shades of red. It's a most extraordinary place."

Tellaga has already touched an extraordinary place in Conred. He is mesmerized. There is something about red…

Tellaga goes on, "The people who lived in Redland were hard workers. The nature of red is action, and act they did! Rest was hard to come by in Redland since everyone overworked. They were always preparing for the next day, making sure they had more than enough. As a matter of fact, they all had too much, and sharing was unheard of. Yet they were proud of their output. They loved to compete with each other to show off how much more they had than their neighbors. But a time came when there was too much smooshed together in Redland, and the people were exhausted. But the red just became more intense and would not let up. They couldn't stop producing even when they were starting to run out of raw materials. They did not know of any other way, so they just kept producing, hoarding, and competing."

"Now Conred, as in all good stories, a unique character appears. In this story it is a young boy. He lived with his family in a pleasant and comfortable home made of the beautiful red clay from the land. But his family had to keep him hidden as there was something different about this boy. It was so different that they feared for his life. The parents had protection in their blood, as the red color dictates, and they wanted to protect their son because of his odd difference. The difference was in his eyes. He had enormous, radiant blue eyes – unheard of in Redland."

"The boy's parents had two reasons to keep him hidden. First, they were afraid of what the town might do to him, since Redlanders always take action. He was so different, and the town never left any issue alone. Secondly, his parents enjoyed the boy for themselves and always wanted him nearby."

"When his father would come home to eat before returning to work for the night shift, he would look across the dinner table and gaze into his son's eyes. The strangest feeling would come over him. He would be aware of that very moment, and no other. And when he was in that moment, he felt his breath, he felt stillness, he felt peace, he felt rest, he felt love for his son, and most surprising, he felt *enough*. There was something his father wanted to do in those moments with his son, something he had never done before or even heard of. He wanted to sit and enjoy the fruits of his labor. And he wanted to give them to others – quite a startling idea! The feeling did not last long, and the father was not sure what this strange new attitude was. He couldn't define it, but he did know that it was new. In these moments, it was hard for the father to get up from the table, but as he glanced away from his son's eyes, the red took over and off he went to work. But there was something different here, too, for when he returned to work, he was renewed – even energized. He had never felt this before."

"His mother also enjoyed gazing into her son's eyes. When she looked into his eyes she felt the moment as well. And in her moment she would step out of her rigidly scheduled mind, away from lists and duties, and step into new places. There were scenes in her mind she had never noticed – a land of make believe. When she stopped looking into her son's blue eyes, she always brought back a new idea from those magical places. But new ideas were not well- thought-of in Redland, because there was no proof they would work, and red must have proof to be safe and continue. The boy's mother would store her ideas in the privacy of her mind. And she, too, would take on the rest of the day with more vitality. She knew she must protect her son at all costs, to keep him, as well as her new way of thinking, safe and sound."

"As their son got older, his eyes got brighter. Blue would shine out of his eyes like headlights. And something else was happening to his parents that they weren't sure how to deal with. Parts of their bodies started to turn blue.

They decided to cover it up with crimson body lotion, but it soon became difficult. The more red they used to cover the blue, the more splotches of purple were on their body – as if the red was taking a beating, and in effect it was. For you see, the more blue they had, the more energy they had. The more energy they had, the more joy they felt. The more joy they felt, the more they let up on their work schedule. The more work they gave up, the more creative they felt. The more creative they felt, the more ideas they had. The more ideas they had, the more ease they felt. The more ease they felt, the more certain they were in the moment. Everything was enough. And this ease gave them more safety and contentment than all the stuff they ever produced. This did not fit in Redland."

"Astonished and awakened, the parents came to a life-changing decision. They decided they would show their own blue skin to the town. They would testify how this new color helped them discover ease in their lives. Ease would be helpful for everyone to use daily with all their hard work. Then, they surmised, once the town was ripe with excitement and curiosity, they would reveal where the blue came from. They would bring their blue-eyed son out of hiding and introduce him to everyone."

"The boy's parents were so excited about this idea. As they were making their plans, something else was stirring inside them, something they had never been aware of before – the concept of sharing. This idea came to them as they were staring into their son's eyes and thinking of the town's welfare – sharing for communal ease! They decided their next step was to call a town meeting. They knew everyone would come, because it would be just one more thing to squeeze into their busy schedules to feel important, and they always did that."

"The father broke the news to his son and excitedly explained, 'At the end of the town meeting, my dear son, we will introduce you to everyone. We will explain the beauty of blue as we show them our skin. The people will start to feel ease. You will be waiting outside by the big red oak tree until your mother comes to get you. Then your beautiful blue eyes will shine down the aisle as you and your mother come towards the podium. The town will then be willing to meet you, perhaps out of curiosity at first. But once they look into your eyes the red will calm, and they will know what we know. They will welcome you.' Then he got more and more excited as he thought where this would lead, 'Perhaps, this ease will help them to start sharing. Perhaps they will share the excess they have, and everyone could start having more ease in their day. This could change the world!' he added eagerly."

"The blue-eyed boy looked adoringly into his father's eyes, and saw a great hero. Then he turned to look at his mother, who always made sure he got a good laugh as he dealt with his difference. He was filled with love for them. The boy was very happy at home, because that was all he knew. Yet now his parents assured him he would be safe to go outside his limits, beyond the gates of his own yard. His excitement grew and grew, as did the intensity of his eyes and the love he felt for his parents. They believed in his difference, and now they were sure others would too! He couldn't wait for the night when he could shine his blue eyes on the town. He was more than ready! How great it was to be different."

"The night arrived for the town meeting. The parents bathed, dried, and for the first time did not cover up the blue patches on their skin. They looked at one another in the red glow of their bedroom, feeling confident as they dressed for the meeting. As they left their bedroom, they took one more glance into each other's eyes and stopped in their tracks. Blue had made its way into their eyes. Their eyes were no longer red, but many shades of iridescent blues. They were delirious with joy and ran to show their son. Their son knew he belonged to them. Needless to say, this was the happiest home in Redland. And the parents realized that tonight would be the perfect time to come out – the family with blue."

"They got into their crimson, four-wheeled carrier and gladly placed their son in the back seat for the first time. As they drove to the town hall, the son enjoyed looking out of the red-tinted windows at all the other homes, playgrounds, stores, and at the river. As they neared their destination, they asked their son to close his eyes so that his glow would be hidden. They walked him to the oak tree in the dark and hid him behind it. 'When you hear the meeting begin you may open your eyes cautiously. Your mother will get you when the time is right for us to introduce you. Son, this is the night we have been waiting for. Just be patient a little longer.' He started to walk away, but then turned back to his son, his eyes glistening with loving moisture, and said, 'My love for you is beyond measure.' And with that, he turned and walked inside."

"The town hall was packed, as expected. The parents walked down the aisle and were greeted with a chorus of 'Is this going to take long?... I still have more to do at home…What's this all about?…I've got another meeting to go to tonight…' and on and on. Such busy people! They walked up to the podium and the father began. As he looked out at the crowd, he noticed that the room was dead silent. He saw jaws dropped and wide-opened red eyes. All in all, it was quite a frozen and speechless audience."

"'My wife and I have gathered you here tonight to share something new and helpful. I see that you are looking at our skin and may notice our eyes as well. This is what we've come here to show you. It is called blue, it's a new color. I know that this is totally opposite of the red you know and live, and it requires a change in your views. But it is something different you will enjoy knowing. We want to give each of you an opportunity to look at our eyes directly so you can understand what this new color can mean for you, for us all…'"

"'Stop!' screamed the woman who owned the biggest red clothing store in town. 'You are sick! What horrible disease do you have that's spreading all over your red skin?' She turned to the crowd, 'It's probably contagious!' The mayor interrupted her, 'Now calm down Myrna. They're up there and we're down here.' But Myrna panicked, 'Dr. Rusty, Dr. Rusty, where are you? We must get these people out of here, get them to the hospital.' The mayor pleaded, trying to maintain control, 'Please, be calm and sit still everyone.'"

"The parents kept going, 'No, we are not sick! Listen to us, let us explain. What we have is good for all of you, and we want to share it with you. It will bring ease to everyone and extra time for all of you to just relax and be yourselves!'"

"The man who owned the Red Car Dealership in town stood up and yelled angrily, 'this red world can't function by relaxing; we've got to be ready. We must always be safe and one step ahead; we must make more than we need. That's what we do. That's what we know. If we are all red and the same, we can compare to see how ahead or behind we are of everyone else. And just what the hell in this big, wide, red world do you mean when you say be yourselves?'"

"The boy's mother responded, 'It's the part of you that's different, the part that wants to come out and really live, to do what you love. It is blue!' She might as well have been talking in a foreign language because they all looked like they had just been freeze-framed. They could not understand these words or this new color. The red audience did not want change. They did not want blue. They did not want to be different. They did not want to be in unknown territory. They did not want to lose their red, and they certainly did not want to get sick with blue. But they *did* want this conversation to end, and they *did* want these blue parents put away, never to come out again."

"'Mayor, you've got to stop them from looking at us, stop this disease. Sheriff, please grab them.' The town hall was redder and hotter than it had ever been. 'Grab those tarps to throw over them; cover their eyes!' bellowed the gym teacher."

'The parents begged them, 'No, stop! You will want what we have. Please, just look into our eyes for a second; just sample what we want to share with you.' They were worried now about the safety of their beautiful boy, who was waiting with such excitement under the tree."

"'Sharing?' exclaimed Rita the librarian, 'Why that is an ancient concept that never worked. You run out of things if you share. And it's hard to tell who is better than whom or who is enough,' she lectured hysterically."

"'It does work, I know it, I feel it!' the father cried, but they were the last words that came out of his mouth, as he and his wife were covered in a tarp and pulled off the stage. They were hauled out of the building and over to the sheriff's car, which was parked next to the big red oak tree. The son sensed something was wrong as he saw the crowd running after, furiously pummeling the two lumps that were under the tarp. And then, as they were being thrown into the Sheriffs car, he saw it. Two tiny, weak blue lights leaking from the tarp."

"The son began to understand that the town was hurting his parents, and his heart broke. He knew he was the reason for all the trouble his parents were in. He suddenly knew of hate. He hated his blue. He hated those people. Fury made a home in him as he ran to the Sheriff's car and beat on the windows. He screamed for his parents – red, blood-curdling screams of pain and loss. The Sheriff's car sped off and the boy ran after it. The crowd followed as well. The boy ran behind the car all the way to the jail. He ran through the angry, red crowd and up to the red officer at the desk. He demanded to see his parents. The officer looked at him and said, 'Parents? What do you mean? Who are you?' he demanded."

"'I am their son,' the boy cried."

"'They don't have a son,' the officer snapped. 'We have enough commotion to deal with around here, now go home.' The boy was shoved out the door. He ran around the back of the building, hoping to find his parents' cell window. He noticed blue coming through one of the windows and climbed up to look inside. He saw his parents holding each other on a small cot. 'Mom, Dad!' he cried to them, and with relief they looked up to see their boy. But when they looked through the window into his eyes, they were destroyed. His beautiful blue eyes were gone; they had become pools of red-hot lava. The parents recoiled into the corner. 'What have we done to our beautiful boy?' they sobbed. They looked back at their child with love and despair. They sank to the floor, closed their blue eyes, and held each other tightly. Then, right before their son's lava eyes, they disappeared from the red earth."

"As he watched his parents leave, the boy's huge love turned into rage. And with red tears pouring from his lava eyes, he uttered a painful cry that echoed through the town. 'No more color!' he screamed. And as the horrible curse left his lips, this precious little boy turned a dull gray. His soft young skin morphed into hard rock, and he grew and grew. 'If color is such an issue for you, I will take them all!

Enjoy your competing and comparing, you fools. You are doomed to gray.'

Right then and there he swore that no one would ever be good enough, no one would ever know their worth, no one would ever be allowed their true colors. He decided to make his world away from others, and for the rest of his life he lived in the air, hovering just out of sight. This provided him with an excellent view so he could make sure he had all colors under control. No one would ever know the joy of what he had with his parents. He had lost them, he had lost his blue, and now the world would do the same."

As Tellaga finishes her story, she notices Conred's eyes flush with red tears. He sobs as buckets and buckets of tears pour down his cheeks. He trembles from the passion and emotion buried in his rock body. His shaking grows into such a loud, vibrating force that it begins to crack his body. Small pieces of rock start dislodging from his arms and legs, followed by larger chunks from his back and chest. Then one final quake of an explosion blows away the remaining rock hard pieces. And left in its wake stands a radiant red boy with beaming, luminous blue eyes, full of love for Tellaga. Tellaga reaches out to him and gazes into his magnificent eyes. She sees the beauty of how uniquely the same we are.

"Mommy, Mommy," Zeal screams as she runs to Tellaga and jumps into her arms. Zeal does not seem to pay much attention to her mother's physical transformation, just the colors, as most children do. "You are sparkly and pink all over Mommy, more than I've ever seen in you before."

Tellaga asks, "Zeal, have you always seen this color in me?"

"Yes, but I couldn't get it out of your gray box." Then Zeal turns to Conred. "Mommy, can I touch him?" Tellaga looks at Conred, the source of all her pain. But before she can give Zeal permission, Zeal eagerly runs to red-and-blue Conred. She cannot wait to get closer to his beautiful colors. Tellaga knows there will be much more between Conred and Zeal.

Since that day Tellaga's life has changed, and she has never been bored again. With compassion and gratitude for Sid's part in her story, Tellaga left him and chose to be around energy that matched her own. Sid is still a lonely workaholic; he is not yet ready to do the math. But Tellaga is not alone. People come from all over, pay her well, and listen to her tell them about their unique stories. They leave with the assignment to figure out the "learning" from their story and to do the math. Once people can hear their drama from the distance of a story, they can leave empowered and able to love their story on their own. They feel as interesting as a good movie. The gift of story – it never ends.

How this book came to be...

Why this book?

The definition of talent is: natural aptitude or skill. Can you identify yours? Many of us think talent only as in a musical prodigy, skillful surgeon, a great painter, successful athlete, etc. But how about the person who can see the best in someone in an instant, or the person who sees the *big* picture with no effort, or the person who is a natural with numbers and solving problems, or the person who is passionate about hiking in the woods, or the 'bossy' person who knows exactly what it takes to get things done, or even the person with a passion for intuition? Do we compare this type of talent to "not as good as"?

It is a fallacy that your talent has to be known by many for it to be worthy in our culture. The purpose of your talent and it being heartfelt for you, is to be able to use it, grow it, and reach out with it...that takes only touching another person.

One of intuition's great skills is to help you discover and guide your unique talent for use in this world. But if you compare the value of your unique talent to that of others, you will not hear this guidance. That is our major block.

We innocently learn to compare from as early as childhood. Be the best, make the most money, look perfect, be popular, be athletic and win, win, win! Comparing should only be used for learning and decision-making not for **self-worth**. Can you feel when that happens in your gut, when comparing slides into making you feel not enough?

My hope is that this fable will help you at the crossroads of comparing for information and to stop at comparing for self worth. To ignite what you deep down love to do by using your talent. When this happens, time flies by and you feel purposeful and want to share your excitement. These are all signs that you are igniting, developing and sharing your talented gift(s).

This fable is for all of us, to discover our own talent, enjoy it, use it, grow with it and offer it to others. If we can role model this, it will help our children enjoy who they are and give them self-confidence in their unique way.

So many children today develop bright new ideas that don't fit in the way we think is "successful". There are many with learning challenges that I have been fortunate enough to have in my life. If they feel loved for who they are and how their talent shows up, then they will find their way. This story of Tellaga and Conred can help do just that.

How I met Tellaga…

A wise person once said, "we teach best what we need to learn". This quote has helped me over and over. Intuition has been my passion since I was a little girl, but I didn't know it had a name.

Fast forward to 49. In the midst of raising and managing a family, owning and operating a business, I realized all along I was helping people and myself make use of our extraordinary inner resource, intuition.

I decided to study in depth how to unleash it. I travelled throughout the USA to learn from some master teachers, endless reading, and many seminars. I eventually found my unique talent on how I was to help others discover their intuition and gifts. I learned intuition knows more that your logical mind. Logic is based on what has already happened. Intuition is from the unknown and knows what best wants to happen, a place for us to create new ideas and solutions.

Intuition knows a bigger picture than what individually we can possibly see. I learned that intuition not only serves the individual, but also the whole when used from the place of truth and love. I learned to welcome the scary unknown... such as writing this book.

Joyce Anderson

After working in the corporate world in my 20's, I felt this is a place where many put their intuition and passion for their talent on hold. It felt stagnating. I discovered that when you listen to your intuition, it knows exactly who, where and what is "out there" that is a perfect match for you. No one other than your intuition knows your hearts desire and what you have to offer. In addition, it's helpful for what's out there that is *not* a match for you. Plus it tells you many times to wait and do nothing, the time is not right. How could we not use this all day long?

I became an Intuition Trainer in 2001 and named my company (per my cute husband's idea) Conversations with YourSelf. I can't tell you all the crazy comments I get about this name. I'm sure you can think of many. However, the name is so much fun and always creates a pause. A laugh and looseness in a person providing fertile ground for intuition to peek through and give a message. I proceeded to give workshops, lectures and individual training. I started writing articles about using intuition in the workplace, even though I never considered myself a 'writer'.

In 2000 I visited an intuitive reader. He looked at me instantly and said "You are a writer." I giggled and said "you must have your wires crossed with my sister. I received terrible grades in English and could never write and follow all those rules. I can't create a story, that is to say, on paper." I was very disappointed in him not telling me something I might like to do! Yet I realized that my conversations were in story form, as I am sure many of you can relate and loved telling them. Another reason I did not want to write is the false thought that writers had to struggle, be moody, and suffer over a typewriter for years... so not my style.

Eventually I decided maybe I could write what 'others' had to say. I researched and found to my delight, several leaders in business who relied heavily on their intuition, even putting intuition before their logical thinking. What a great non-fiction book this could be, and it would help the 8 – 5 working world that was so starved to use their intuition.

I conducted my first interview with a woman who ran an international company based in High Point, NC. Not only did she put intuition first, but purposely filtered that idea through her company. It was amazing to walk into this manufacturing plant and feel the importance of every one who worked there, no matter what their job title. I then interviewed a few more.

When I sat down to write these amazing interviews, I kept dragging my feet. Months went by. I was procrastinating on this book that I said I was going to write. It made logical sense for me to write this book. To record these leaders' words for people to learn from, very noble I felt. My logic would pretend I was excited about this, yet I was less and less so, certainly never admitting it.

Tellaga had something else in mind. One day as I was forcing myself to sit at the computer and write this darn book, I caught myself staring out the window. I was daydreaming about of a few clients I was coaching who were so mad at themselves for their weight challenges. A disturbing and odd image came to my mind. I started seeing these lovely clients with excess weight deciding to pop out of their body leaving gaping holes in their arms, legs and torsos. They then started shining and smiling, even as their holes were very painful.

I tried to snap myself out of this imagery and then thought, hello, this is intuition speaking, sit with this message...and then came Tellaga. This beautiful pink creature appeared in that deep place within me. Next I saw the letters of her name. I felt excitement, turned to my computer and began typing a fictional story.

I had to fight my logical mind not to compare myself to other writers. I had to fight Conred who said, "You're 55, you have never been a writer. You don't know how, you've got a marketing degree, not an English degree. You can't create any thing new, just stick to what others have said, and do the interviews...on and on."

At that moment, with Conred, I felt small and hard, I missed the way I felt when I had Tellaga in my heart. With her I felt alive, full, attentive, productive and not wanting to stop. I decided to keep Tellaga with me the whole time. It seemed as if my life came to this wonderful point, where there were no mistakes from the past, just learning's to go into this tapestry.

This story turned out very different than when I first started. The first attempt was too filled with Conred remarks trying to hard to become an author. With two dear writer friends input, Linda and Gabriel, I decided to begin a second time. I would not let my rational and/or critical mind take over, but let Tellaga/intuition be my guide. This book took two years to write due to life's ups and downs, plus a move from the Southeast to the Northwest.

What I learned was to go to the learning from a situation I was not settled with. With this new learning, I would sit at my computer and have Tellaga guide my words through the pages. I would keep at bay how many days went by, and allow no time-guilt to whittle away my newly loved creativity.

Having no drawing ability, it was so important to find the right illustrator. Letting intuition help and having wonderful friends, old and new, I was led to the amazing Liz Gill Neilson. Liz created the cover and illustrations that had found a home in my imagination. It's as if Tellaga had visited Liz as well. This book taught me to reach out and ask for help. How silly, as if we are supposed to create alone. We can never be great alone.

I am so in love with this book and those who touched it. This book is the type you read over and over again, to learn deeper and deeper. I giggle and keep wondering who wrote this? I always learn something more when I read it again.

With love, I hope you recognize Conred and the other archetypes in this book so you can stop the comparing when it happens. There is as archetype section at the end of this book that will help you. Tellaga and Agatha will help you recover your talents and put them to use. May you say goodbye to self-critical and hello to self-thrilled.

Joyce Anderson

How you can work
with these archetypes:

Archetypes, Our Interior Characters

By Joyce Anderson, Conversations with YourSelf
www.conversationswithyourself.com

Definition of an archetype: a collectively inherited unconscious idea, pattern of thought, and image universally present in individual psyches. They are interesting characters we all share. Archetypes can help to lighten up a situation, help with humor and safe distance to understand what's going on. Usually, we first see them in others before we see them in ourselves. For example, I know a woman who uses Conred way too much! She in turn pushes my Conred button. Being aware of this, I can switch to Tellaga to deal with Conred. To reiterate, archetypes are universally present.

Look at your life in story form. Can you see the archetypes listed below in your life? When you read each one:

- What color pops into your head? What personal color feels right for you when reading each archetype? Note that color. Use it when thinking about the archetypes. There is energy in color.

- Look deep into the images below. You may use them, or allow your imagination to create your own. Their traits are universal, but their images can be as unique as you. Remember, we are uniquely the same.

- Continue by listing some of the times and events when these archetypes are obvious in your life. Call them by name and note only your feelings.

- Then go back and write next to the feelings, what was the teaching that archetype was there to help you learn. For example, if you felt empty, what do you think that archetype was there to teach you?

- No blaming others allowed. When something deeply annoys you about someone else, that something is deep in you. Archetypes help push that button. What is that archetype's message for you?

- Play with them. Let them be fun and humorous for you. Humor allows for objectivity and greater viewing for making effective choices.

Archetype personalities signal you in many ways such as: energetic or lazy, creative or stagnant, friendly or lonely, active or procrastinating, victim or controlling, offering or hoarding your skills, feeling large or small, gray or colorful, etc. Use these archetypes for quick identification of what's going on. Listen to them and challenge them.

What is their message to you? What do you need to learn? Then turn to your highest intuitive self, your inner GPS, for wisdom on your next step. In the book, Tellaga says "When stuck, do to the opposite."

TELLAGA, HIGHEST INTUITIVE SELF:

Tellaga is the creative energy that knows how to use your best skills for what wants to happen. It knows what person, place and idea is a match for the best you.

Description:

- Feels wise and relaxed deep in your core
- Connects to the bigger picture and knows how you fit in
- Color-full, feels open and light
- Creativity, welcomes the 'new'
- Face everything, fear nothing
- Gives steps one at a time
- **Goal: To evolve individually for the whole.**

ZEAL, THE GAS FOR LIFE:

Zeal is the energy of fascination. Zeal is the spirit within that knows there is no better or worse; just wonder about learning, giving and connecting. Thrilled that about being 'uniquely the same'.

Description:

- Feels effervescent in skin

- Childlike wonder
- Moves forward, action filled
- No limits, can't wait to explore
- Excited to use talents
- Creates with others
- **Goal: Taking action to engage.**

YOUNG AGATHA:

Agatha is the energy of lovability and vulnerability, born to interact in this dynamic, crazy world. Vulnerable is the faith to remain open. Young Agatha plays, says and imagines being anything she wishes. She loves being herself in the world to daydream with others.

Description:

- Feels grounded and confident
- Loveable and vulnerable
- Daydreaming, pretending and believing
- Playing with friends, singing, dancing, games, sports, crafting, coloring, etc.
- **Goal: Do what you love, share and play**

Y.C. – (Why See) YOUNG CONRED:

Y.C. is the energy of bravery and faith. His blue eyes see we are uniquely the same. His bravery comes from engaging in his difference for the sake of all. He sees the importance of each unique life, and its importance to heal the world.

Description:

- Feels strong in body
- Head believes in guidance from the heart
- Courage to speak and act not knowing the outcome
- Brave with originality
- **Goal: Bravery to make a difference.**

AGATHA: NEUTRAL LIFE.

Agatha is the energy of passivity, just getting by. Agatha passes over her importance and her gut instinct. She is barely 15% of her brilliant full self. Bottles up her talents, wishes and words and has trouble offering or receiving anything of value.

Agatha puts others before her.

Description:

- Feels controlled, rote, replaceable, dragging
- Low self-esteem, no zeal
- 'Should" runs her life, lives by others demands
- Complacent , time watcher
- Bottles up wishes and desires
- Surface conversations
- Lifestyle hurts health
- **Goal: Be passive, don't really count**

CONRED, KING OF COMPARISON:

Conred is the energy of comparing for self-worth using the past. He thrives on sucking the colors and originality right out of you with hurtful past episodes. He amplifies hurt and guilt for being you.

Description:

- Feels heavy, closed, gray, sunken heart
- Dooming future, hates new and different
- Compares for self-worth

- Sucks energy from others
- Uses blame and the past
- Buries originality
- Constant brain dialog: Better than/less than, not enough/too much
- **Goal: Compare for self-worth, for then there will be none.**

SOLDIERS OF COMPARISON:

These soldiers represent the energy of not belonging. The soldiers in your head use groups to prove you are 'not enough' or 'better than' to belong. Soldiers  push you to join groups of 'same' that are formed to keep 'different' out. Then you have a sense of special belonging. Once in this group of two or many, the army of comparing grows. Your group must win, must be better than. The truth is we all belong; the soldiers believe only some belong. The result is war from inside to out. Are you in a group that's open to others or closed?

- Feel judged, longing to be included & understood, on edge
- Either in or out

116

- Need to compare in conversations
- Depend on others approval
- Surround yourself with 'like' comparers
- Must win for proof of superiority
- **Goal: Either in or out, then war**

COATES:

The energy of hiding. Think of when you got your first dose of hurt feelings? Being young, you thought being 'you' was the cause. Out of self-preservation and not knowing any better, a protective energy begins. You desire something from the world that feels good, since people have hurt. Addictions are something from the outside that go inside to help you bury your hurt, consistently. What form of hiding do you use? What addiction describes your Coates?

Description:

- Feel suffocated, stifled, numb, hands around throat, eyes seem small
- Form of coats: food, alcohol, drugs, internet, TV, workaholic, over-involved, etc.
- Covers voice and desire

- Hides the talent you love the most
- **Goal: Safety in hiding, no one can hurt**

SID, SABOTAGING YOUR IDENTITY:

Sid is the energy of victimhood, giving the responsibility of who you are to others. When you don't see yourself as unique for the positive, you give the job of directing your days to a Sid. Then you don't have to be brave and responsible for your choices. Once you identify your Sid, it's your courage of who you are that can release anyone you have assigned the job of sabotaging your id.

Description:

- Feeling pulled, scheduled, anchored, no choice
- Find yourself saying, I can't because of "(insert)"
- Doing only what is expected, can't step into a new idea
- Owns abilities you think you don't
- Out of your hands, feel incapable
- **Goal: Give up responsibility for your wishes and talent.**

Reading Group Suggestions

1. Set a goal to delete 'comparision' words during your meeting: Example: the ***most*** beautiful, and convert it to <u>a</u> beautiful. See what your meeting is like when you take out comparison words in everyday conversation.

2. Ask each other to describe their characteristics when they are in full color. How could they use these skills everyday regardless of their job/or daily chores?

3. In a circle, start with one person who will speak to the person on the right. Mention a talent they see in that person. This could be an intuitive knowing or something they have witnessed about that person. Continue the circle.

4. Discuss Conred. How does he show up in your life? Where are you stuck on ***not encouraging too much or less than better than?***

5.   Discuss Sid. He stands for Sabotaging your ID, (S.ID). Discuss one of your SID's. A person, job, busyness, or addiction you attracted to show you where you are not being you. Finish your conversation with "I am enough."

6.   Discuss Redland where Conred was born. Is part of your life covered in red. How could you introduce blue into this part of your life?

7.   Discuss Coates. Has there been a long time friend like Coates that you have used to cover up? Is it time to say thank you and take off Coates? What does taking off Coates signify? Share your story if you have already done this.

8.   Tellaga represents your higher intuitive knowledge. Share a time when your Tellaga helped you. Give a name to your Tellaga.

9.   Conred comes full circle from the villain to the redeemed one. What does this say to you?

10. On page 83 Tellaga gives her math equation "a negative X a negative = a positive"; do the math with a personal example of this and share.

11. I once read a quote about zeal: "I am now filled with divine Zeal. I move toward my highest good. Through the spirit within, my enthusiasm for life and living is boundless." How does Zeal in the book relate to this definition? What stages does Agatha go through to reconnect to her zeal?

Joyce Anderson

Years ago while owning and operating a Jazzercise franchise, raising children, and managing a family, Joyce was haunted by an unfulfilled part stirring inside. By talking with others it was apparent that sensation also haunted many...if not all of us. Her explorations taught her that much of the void was not in what we didn't have, but that we were not making use of what we do have...our inner resource known as intuition that helps us guide and use our unique talent.

Her passion for her children, and experience in raising a brilliant child with learning disabilities taught her the necessity of recognizing, encouraging and using their unique talent. No matter what challenges you have, Joyce learned how you can transform your self-criticism to being self-thrilled by liking and using your unique 'thumbprint'; and how to engage and take direction from your intuitive wisdom.

Her latest work is **Silent Parenting©**. **Silent Parenting©** begins with your silent beliefs and worries that you carry in your heart for your child, before the words even come out of your mouth. This translates in to fear for them and affects their self-confidence. Children are like sponges and pick up this silent worry and then doubt themselves. ***Silent Parenting*©** starts with role modeling. Parents and teachers identify their own unique talent and passions so they can teach the child to do the same. Your worried beliefs change to optimistic beliefs for your child. Children learn by what we do and what we believe, not what we preach. If you role model what you want them to be, your words and teaching become effective, as does their self-confidence.

Joyce Anderson is an Intuition Educator. In 2001 she began Conversations with YourSelf. Through her radio show: *Conversations with YourSelf*, keynotes, workshops, individual training and writings she has taught many the use of practical intuition in everyday life. She is the author of published articles on using intuition in the workplace. She has a B.A. in Marketing from Florida International University and lives in Seattle, Washington. Visit www.conversationswithyourself.com.

Liz Gill Neilson

Liz Gill Neilson is a painter, printmaker, and designer. Liz hails from the Boston area, received her B.A. in visual arts from Columbia University, NYC, and now lives in Portland, Oregon. In her work, she strives to create a mythology of form that reveals the web of connection between humans and the natural world. Liz is the Artist in Residence for the Portland Chamber Orchestra, and creates multi-arts projects for the PCO and other music ensembles across the country, bringing visual art, animation and story into concert settings. She also works as an illustrator and graphic designer, designing books, albums, and other print media for artists and organizations. Liz's work is represented by The Gallery Zero in Portland. Visit her website at www.lizgillneilson.com.